Introduction

Developing Skills for Writing
Supporting Children to Achieve Level 3
by Sue Garnett

Developing Skills for Writing Level 3 is a resource to help busy teachers raise standards in writing from the English National Curriculum Level 3 to Level 4 (approximate ages 7 to 9). The activities cover work on verbs, punctuation, connectives, adjectives, adverbs, prepositions and noun phrases at an appropriate level. The activities focus mainly on sentence level work with some opportunities for text level work. Where possible, optional worksheets are available with a focus on boys' interests. Step by step lesson plans explain clearly how the activities are to be carried out. The photocopiable pages can be used with whole classes, small groups or individual pupils at the discretion of the class teacher. All photocopiable pages have been printed in 'landscape' to make maximum use of the space on interactive whiteboards. Lesson plans are written in a simple style for teaching assistants to use when working with an individual or small group. 'Helping Hands' are used at the end of each lesson to record simply what has been learnt.

Topical Resources
P.O. Box 329
Broughton
Preston
Lancashire
England
PR3 5LT

Topical Resources publishes a range of Educational Materials for use in Primary Schools and Pre-School Nurseries and Playgroups.

For latest catalogue:
Tel: 01772 863158
Fax: 01772 866153

E.mail: sales@topical-resources.co.uk
Visit our Website on:
www.topical-resources.co.uk

Copyright @ Sue Garnett

Illustrated by John Hutchinson, Art Works, Fairhaven, 69 Worden Lane, Leyland, Preston PR5 2BD

Designed by Paul Sealey, PS3 Creative, 3 Wentworth Drive, Thornton, Lancashire

Printed in the UK for 'Topical Resources' by T. Snape and Co Ltd., Boltons Court, Preston, Lancashire

First Published September 2011
ISBN 978-1-907269-63-9

Contents

Verbs
Lesson 1 – Lesson Plan .
    Worksheet 1
    Worksheet 2
    Worksheet 3a
    Worksheet 3b . . . . Page 6
Lesson 2 – Lesson Plan . . . . Page 7
    Worksheet 1 . . . . Page 8
    Worksheet 2 . . . . Page 9
    Worksheet 3 . . . . Page 10

Punctuation
Lesson 1 – Lesson Plan . . . . Page 11
    Worksheet 1a . . . . Page 12
    Worksheet 1b . . . . Page 13
    Worksheet 2 . . . . Page 14
Lesson 2 – Lesson Plan . . . . Page 15
    Worksheet 1 . . . . Page 16
    Worksheet 2 . . . . Page 17
Lesson 3 – Lesson Plan . . . . Page 18
    Worksheet 1 . . . . Page 19
    Worksheet 2 . . . . Page 20
Lesson 4 – Lesson Plan . . . . Page 21
    Worksheet 1 . . . . Page 22
    Worksheet 2 . . . . Page 23
    Worksheet 3 . . . . Page 24

Connectives
Lesson 1 – Lesson Plan . . . . Page 25
    Worksheet 1 . . . . Page 26
    Worksheet 2 . . . . Page 27
    Worksheet 3 . . . . Page 28
    Worksheet 4 . . . . Page 29
Lesson 2 – Lesson Plan . . . . Page 30
    Worksheet 1 . . . . Page 31
    Worksheet 2 . . . . Page 32
Lesson 3 – Lesson Plan . . . . Page 33
    Worksheet 1 . . . . Page 34
    Worksheet 2 . . . . Page 35
    Worksheet 3 . . . . Page 36
Lesson 4 – Lesson Plan . . . . Page 37
    Worksheet 1 . . . . Page 38
    Worksheet 2 . . . . Page 39
    Worksheet 3 . . . . Page 40

Adjectives
Lesson 1 – Lesson Plan . . . . Page 41
    Worksheet 1 . . . . Page 42
    Worksheet 2 . . . . Page 43
    Worksheet 3 . . . . Page 44
    Worksheet 4 . . . . Page 45
Lesson 2 – Lesson Plan . . . . Page 46
    Worksheet 1 . . . . Page 47
    Worksheet 2 . . . . Page 48

Adverbs
Lesson 1 – Lesson Plan . . . . Page 49
    Worksheet 1 . . . . Page 50
    Worksheet 2 . . . . Page 51
    Worksheet 3 . . . . Page 52
Lesson 2 – Lesson Plan . . . . Page 53
    Worksheet 1 . . . . Page 54
    Worksheet 2 . . . . Page 55
    Worksheet 3 . . . . Page 56

Prepositions
Lesson 1 – Lesson Plan . . . . Page 57
    Worksheet 1 . . . . Page 58
    Worksheet 2 . . . . Page 59
    Worksheet 3 . . . . Page 60

Noun Phrases
Lesson 1 – Lesson Plan . . . . Page 61
    Worksheet 1 . . . . Page 62
    Worksheet 2 . . . . Page 63

Additional Resources . . . . Pages 64 - 69

Level 3 - Verbs (Irregular): Lesson 1

Writing Focus: Sentence Structure & Punctuation   **Theme:** Recount - A Day Out

Target	To use irregular verbs in the past tense
Resources	Worksheets, 'Helping Hand' card (page 64) Irregular Verbs (see pages 65 and 66).
Warm Up	Words canyou make out of the word - INVESTIGATED ?
Introduction	**Objective:** • Today we are looking at verbs in the past tense which are irregular i.e. you don't add 'ed' **By the end of the lesson:** • You will be able to spell irregular verbs in the past tense with their correct spellings. • You will be able to use the verbs in your own sentences.
Remember	Reminder and reinforcement of key learning from previous lesson (if appropriate).
Model/Try	1. **Card Game** Remaind children that verbs are doing words. (N.B. Irregular verbs do not follow a particular spelling pattern when they are changed to past tense.) Lay out the irregular verbs in the present tense. Pick up the irregular verbs in the past tense. Match them up with the present tense and then say them out loud. If more able, say out loud the past tense of the irregular verbs and then write them down without looking a second time. Correct any mistakes. 2. **Sentence Game** Turn the irregular past tense cards face down. In turn, pick up a word and make a sentence out loud. To make it more difficult, pick up two words and think of a sentence. 3. **Worksheet 1: Verb Game** Each child to have a copy of Worksheet 1. First the teacher writes an irregular verb in the present tense e.g. bring. Child/children to spell the past tense of the word on a wipe board. If they get it right, they can write the word on the pictures. If they don't, write the word correctly for them and then they can write it down. 4. **Worksheet 2: Word Search** Find the irregular verbs.
Apply	5. **Write a Report** Look at Worksheet 3a 'Day at the Seaside' or 3b 'At the Match.' Fill in the spaces with the correct spelling of the irregular verbs.
Secure	6. Read through your work. 7. Choose some of the irregular verbs you have used and spell them without looking.
Review & Reflect	8. Write some of the irregular verbs in the past tense onto a 'Helping Hand' card.

Name: _____ Date: _____

Irregular Verbs

Level 3 – Verbs: Lesson 1 - Worksheet 1

Write the past tense of given verbs on the pictures.

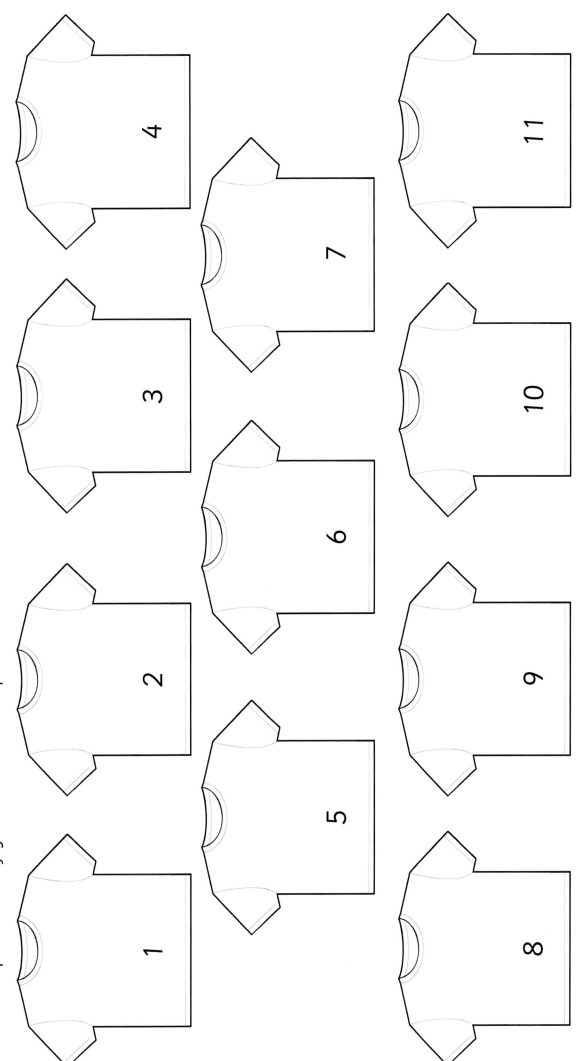

Name: _____ Date: _____

Word Search
Find the irregular verbs.

Level 3 - Verbs: Lesson 1 - Worksheet 2

ACROSS
thought
woke
dug
found
bought

DOWN
threw
fell
caught
heard
brought

t	h	o	u	g	h	t	b
h	x	w	u	w	e	i	r
r	b	f	z	q	a	c	o
e	z	i	x	m	r	a	u
w	o	k	e	f	d	u	g
f	o	u	n	d	k	g	h
e	l	b	o	u	g	h	t
l	z	w	o	n	z	t	v
l	o	k	v	d	z	o	x

Irregular Verbs in Sentences

Fill in the spaces with the correct spelling of the irregular verbs.

A Day at the Seaside

Last week, my mum, brother and I _____ (go) to the seaside. We _____ (wake) up early and _____ (catch) the train. My mum _____ (bring) a picnic.

First we walked along the sea front. My mum _____ (take) us to a rock shop and she _____ (buy) us some rock. I _____ (eat) it all before we got home. After that I _____ (drink) some lemonade.

In the afternoon we went on the beach. I _____ (fly) my kite. I _____ (run) along the beach with it. My little brother _____ (ride) a donkey. I _____ (find) a £1 coin on the sand. We played with a beach ball. I _____ (throw) the ball to my little brother. Then I _____ (swim) in the sea and I _____ (see) lots of little fish. My brother _____ (lose) his dummy in the sea when he was paddling. My mum _____ (stand) by the water's edge. I _____ (write) a post card to my Grandma.

On the way back to the station my brother _____ (fall) but he didn't hurt himself. When we got home, I _____ (tell) my friend about our day out. I was so tired I _____ (sleep) for twelve hours!

Name: _____ Date: _____

Irregular Verbs in Sentences

Fill in the spaces with the correct spelling of the irregular verbs.

The Football Match

Last Saturday, my dad and I _____ (go) to watch my town football team. I _____(wake) up early and after lunch we _____ (catch) the bus to the ground. First I _____ (buy) a scarf. Next we _____(stand) in the queue and then we went through the turnstile. We _____(find) our seats, sat down and then the match _____ (begin). My dad _____ (bring) some sweets for us to eat.

At half time my dad _____ (take) me to the café and he _____ (buy) me a pie. I _____(eat) it all before we got back to our seats. I _____ (drink) some lemonade too.

The other team played well and I _____(think) we would lose but five minutes before the end we scored. The goal keeper _____(throw) the ball to the defender who passed it to the winger. He _____(fly) down the pitch to the corner flag and _____(take) on the left back. Then he crossed the ball. The striker _____ (run) towards him and the goalie reached out for the ball and _____(fall) over. Calmly, the striker tapped the ball into the net. We _____(stand) up and cheered. We_____(win) the game 1 - 0. The other team hadn't _____(lose) at all this season and so we were really happy.

After the game we _____ (stand) outside and waited for the players. I _____ (see) all of the team. The striker _____ (write) his name in my autograph book. That evening I _____ (hear) that the goalie _____ (break) his ankle. The next day I _____(tell) my friends about the match.

6

Level 3 - Verbs (Powerful): Lesson 2

Writing Focus: Sentence Structure & Punctuation   **Theme:** Non-Fiction Diary

Target	To use powerful verbs in writing including other verbs for 'went'
Resources	Worksheets, marker pens, scissors, cube and 'Helping Hand' card (see page 64), Powerful Verb cards (page 67).
Warm Up	How many words can you make out of the word - POWERFUL?
Introduction	**Objective:** • Today we are going to learn how to use powerful verbs to improve our writing. • We are going to focus on the word 'went' and find out what alternatives there are. **By the end of the lesson:** • You will be able to use powerful verbs in your writing.
Remember	Reminder and reinforcement of key learning from previous lesson (if appropriate).
Model/Try	1. **Verb Cards** Cut up the verb cards. Read the powerful verb cards (alternative words for 'went'). Explain any words that the child doesn't understand e.g. hobbled etc. 2. **Act it Out** Cut up the cards. Turn them face down. Take it in turns to choose a word and act it out e.g. crawled. 3. **Worksheet 1: Matching Game** Look at the pictures on Worksheet 1. Match the powerful verb cards to the pictures. 4. **Worksheet 2: Example Texts** Read version 1 of the story 'Colby's Diary'. Then read version 2 'Harry's Diary'. What do you notice about the two diaries? Version 1 (poor example) It is boring because - • Not enough information. • Sentences are all the same length, which makes it uninteresting. • Sentences begin with the same words i.e. the boy's name or a pronoun. • The word 'went' is used a lot and there are no powerful verbs. Version 2 (good example) It is interesting and exciting because - • Lots of information. • Sentences are different lengths. • Sentences begin with different words e.g. nouns, verbs. • Powerful verbs used e.g. skidded. 5. **Activity 4: Cube Game** Choose six of the powerful verbs and write them on a cube. Take it in turns to roll the cube and think of a sentence using that word. Then choose another six and play the game again.
Apply	6. **Worksheet 3: Write Sentences** Look at Worksheet 3. Write your own diary about an outdoor activity holiday using powerful verbs.
Review & Reflect	7. **Helping Hand** Choose five powerful verbs you would like to start using in your writing and write them on the 'Helping Hand'.

7

Name: _____ Date: _____

Powerful Verbs

Match the powerful verb cards to the pictures.

Level 3 – Verbs: Lesson 2 - Worksheet 1

© Topical Resources. May be photocopied for classroom use only.

Name: _____ Date: _____

Adventure Diaries

Read the two diaries.
What is different about them?

Colby's Diary

Monday 1st July
I'm writing my diary at Cockleshell Adventure Centre. I've come here with my class. This afternoon we **went** rock climbing.

Tuesday 2nd July
We **went** on the moors. We **went** fast for the first three miles. After lunch we had to find our way back.

Wednesday 3rd July
We **went** to the seaside. We **went** off the rocks into the water. Tom did a belly flop.

Thursday 4th July
We **went** to some caves. We **went** on our hands and knees.

Friday 5th July
We **went** biking. Jack fell off his bike. Tomorrow we are going home. I will be sad.

Harry's Diary

Monday 1st July
I'm writing this diary while sitting on my bunk bed at Cockleshell Adventure Centre. I've come here with my class for six whole days! The first day has been brilliant. After lunch, we **climbed** some steep rocks at High Grove. It was brilliant.

Tuesday 2nd July
Today we **hiked** across the moors. Our instructor made us **march** the first three miles which was exhausting! After lunch he taught us how to read maps and then we had to find our own way back. My team **jogged** all the way and we came second.

Wednesday 3rd July
I felt really tired today because we had a pillow fight last night until two o'clock! In the afternoon we took the cliff path to the sea. We had a lot of fun especially when we **jumped** off the rocks into the water. Tom stumbled over a rock and did a belly flop into the water which made everyone laugh!

Thursday 4th July
I had a brilliant day. We drove to some caves. It was pitch black and very scary. We were given helmets and wetsuits. We **crawled** through the caves on our hands and knees. We were soaked to the skin!

Friday 5th July
We were given mountain bikes this morning and we had to ride as fast as we could down a rocky path. Jack **skidded** and came off his bike because he was going so fast. He twisted his ankle and he limped all the way back to the centre. Tomorrow morning we are going home. It's been a brilliant week! I've enjoyed writing my diary too!

Level 3 – Verbs: Lesson 2 - Worksheet 2

© Topical Resources. May be photocopied for classroom use only.

Name: _____
Date: _____

My Holiday Diary

Write your own diary about an adventure holiday using powerful verbs.

hiked   crawled   leapt   climbed   skidded

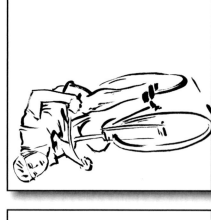

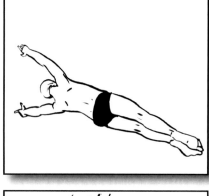

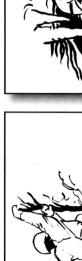

Day 1

Day 2

Day 3

Level 3 - Punctuation (Speech Marks): Lesson 1

Writing Focus: Sentence Structure & Punctuation   **Theme:** Report

Target	To use speech marks
Resources	Worksheets, highlighter pens.
Warm Up	**Egg Timer Game** How many words can you make using the word 'PUNCTUATION' e.g. pat, put, pit, cat, cot, tan, tin, ton, not, nut, ant etc.
Introduction	**Objective:** • Today we are going to learn how to use speech marks with the correct layout and punctuation. **By the end of the lesson:** • You will be able to use speech marks in a newspaper report.
Remember	Reminder and reinforcement of key learning from previous lesson (if appropriate).
Model/Try	1. **Speech Marks** Draw some speech marks for the child/children. Explain that these are speech marks and when we see them in writing it means that someone is talking. (Show examples from a real newspaper, magazine or storybook etc.) 2. **News Reports** Choose Worksheet 1a or 1b. Read out loud Text 1. Explain that this text is a news report. Explain that people usually make comments in a news report. Explain that we need the speech marks otherwise the reader will not know when someone is speaking. Draw coloured circles around the speech marks. Highlight the words that were spoken. Using the speech bubbles, write the words that the people said and then who said the words underneath the bubbles. 3. **Classroom Conversation** Worksheet 1a or 1b. Read out loud Text 2. Explain that this conversation is missing speech marks. Explain that along with the speech marks, we need extra punctuation marks. We can either use a comma, question mark or exclamation mark before the last speech mark. Put in the speech marks and other punctuation. (If they cannot do this easily, explain the last set of speech marks will come before the words: said, asked, replied, answered or shouted.) Also notice that when someone different speaks, we start a new line.
Apply	4. **Worksheet 2: The Daily Record** Read the news report. Make up comments that could have been given by the people involved in the story i.e. the boy, the mother, the vet, RSPCA, the police. Before you begin to write, say out loud what you think that person would say. Remember to start a new line when someone speaks. Use the correct punctuation when the person finishes speaking.
Secure	5. Highlight the speech marks in the report and the punctuation.
Review & Reflect	6. Write the rules for using speech marks on a 'Helping Hand' card.

Name: _____ Date: _____

Speech Marks

Circle the speech marks. Highlight the words spoken. Write what was spoken in the speech bubbles. Label who spoke each speech bubble. Finally, punctuate the classroom conversation.

NEWS REPORT — Text 1

It's raining money!

In the small town of Hardwick, shoppers were treated to free money on Saturday when a man on the roof of the bank emptied a suitcase full of money onto the shoppers below. Shoppers picked up over £20,000 but most of it was handed into the police who arrived on the scene in minutes.

"It was raining money," said Sally Carr, aged 21.

"I picked up £100!" said ten year old Harry Jones.

"The pavement was covered in £10 notes," said John Brand, the bank manager.

Police are looking for a tall grey haired man, with glasses.

CLASSROOM CONVERSATION — Text 2

Harry Jones was telling his friends at school about the mystery money.

How much money did you get asked Jake

£100   answered Harry.

Cool   shouted Jake.

Did you give it back asked Lisa

Yes, we handed it over to the police replied Harry.

Name: _____ Date: _____

Speech Marks

Level 3 – Punctuation: Lesson 1 - Worksheet 1b

Circle the speech marks. Highlight the words spoken. Write what was spoken in the speech bubbles. Label who spoke each speech bubble. Finally, punctuate the classroom conversation.

Text 1

NEWS REPORT
Neston United 3 Hardwick Rovers 0

Neston United players danced with joy after they beat Hardwick Rovers 3 - 0 in the Cup Final. A 23rd-minute goal set Neston on their way with a powerful shot from Luke Wilson. In the second half Jack Grant made the score 2 - 0 with a diving header. In the last minute of the second half young Adam Jones scored his first goal for the club. At the final whistle, the players had a group hug as the supporters went wild in the stands.

"The team was amazing," said Ray Barnes the manager.

"The best team won," said Jack Grant the captain.

"It's been the best day of my life," said Adam Jones.

Text 2

CLASSROOM CONVERSATION

Harry King went to the cup final. He was telling his friends at school about it.

What was the score asked Jake

3-0 to Neston answered Harry.

Cool shouted Jake.

Did you get any autographs asked Anna.

No, but I shook hands with the captain replied Harry.

Wow! I wish I'd been there said Anna.

Name: _____ Date: _____

The Daily Record

Make up comments that could have been given by the people involved in the story.

10th September 2011 - WHEELIE BIN PUPPIES

A boy of ten has saved the lives of six tiny puppies which had been left to die in a wheelie bin in the town of Bentham.

Karl Smith found the puppies in a wheelie bin near his home. He'd been playing in the garden when the ball had gone over the fence. Climbing over the fence, he had heard whimpering sounds coming from a wheelie bin near the bus shelter. To his surprise, inside the bin were three tiny Jack Russell puppies. He took the puppies home and his mother called the RSPCA. They took the puppies to the vet to be checked over. They were under weight and had sore eyes but with some tender loving care they have been brought back to health. For saving their lives, Karl's mother let him keep one. Since the incident, the police have spoken to over one hundred families in the neighbourhood, but they have still to find out who did this dreadful thing.

_____

_____

_____

_____

Level 3 – Punctuation: Lesson 1 - Worksheet 2

Level 3 - Punctuation (Speech Marks): Lesson 2

Writing Focus: Sentence Structure & Punctuation **Theme:** Conversation

Target	To use speech marks with increased accuracy.
Resources	Worksheets, highlighter pens, 'Helping Hand' cards (page 64.)
Warm Up	**I went to market** Play I went to market. You could develop the theme by being specific e.g. items for a birthday party; items to go on holiday etc.
Introduction	**Objective:** • Today we are going to develop speech marks and use them in our writing. **By the end of the lesson:** • You will be able to use speech marks and different words for 'said' in conversation.
Remember	Reminder and reinforcement of key learning from previous lesson (if appropriate).
Model/Try	1. **Worksheet 1 - Story** These stories are set during World War 2 when children were evacuated to the countryside because the cities were being bombed. It is a conversation between the evacuees and the children who live in the countryside. Read Text 1 (without any speech marks.) Now read Text 2 (with speech marks) What is the difference? Text 2 has speech marks. Discuss what makes Text 2 easier to read and understand than Text 1? Point out it has speech marks to tell us when someone is speaking. What is the difference in layout between Text 1 and Text 2? In Text 2 a new line is always started when someone new speaks. How does this help the reader? Answer: It shows the reader that someone else will be speaking. Look at Text 2 again. Highlight the punctuation used with the speech marks. What choice of punctuation can you use after speech marks? Answer: comma, question mark or exclamation mark. 2. **Worksheet 1: Different Words for 'Said** Highlight the different words for 'said' i.e. asked, replied, shouted. 3. **Worksheet 2: Story** Read the text and then put in speech marks and punctuation. Highlight other words for 'said'.
Apply	4. **Worksheet 2: New Child in the Class.** Write your own conversation between two children, one who has been at the school a while and the other who is a new child. Work in twos. Before you write anything down, act out the conversation with your partner. Afterwards write down the conversation. e.g. "What's your name?" asked Alice Use speech marks, punctuation, and different words for said and start a new line when someone speaks. Set the scene first before you start the conversation e.g. Rebecca was new to Y4. At play time the teacher asked Alice to look after her. Rebecca and Alice sat on the bench and began to chat.
Secure	5. Read through your conversation. Edit. Highlight the speech marks and punctuation.
Review & Reflect	6. How many rules can you think of when using speech in your writing? Write your rules on the 'Helping Hand' cards. Write down alternatives for the word 'said'.

15

Name: _____   Date: _____

World War 2 Stories

Read the texts and compare how they are written.

Home in the Country — Text 1

It was the 1st September 1939. England was at war. Mary aged 10 and Oliver aged 5 had been sent to the countryside from London. Oliver was frightened because he had never been away from his parents. When they arrived at the cottage, they were greeted by two girls aged 10 and 7. Hello, I'm Grace said the 10 year old girl. I'm Agnes said the 7 year old girl. I'm Mary and this is Oliver replied Mary. Have you come a long way asked Grace? About 100 miles said Mary. That's a long way said Agnes. Come inside now said their mother. We've got scones with jam said Agnes. Is it strawberry jam asked Oliver? Yes replied Grace. Brilliant shouted Oliver, beginning to smile.

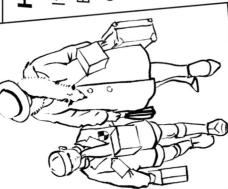

Home in the Country — Text 2

It was the 1st September 1939. England was at war. Mary aged 10 and Oliver aged 5 had been sent to the countryside from London. Oliver was frightened because he had never been away from his parents.

When they arrived at the cottage, they were greeted by two girls aged 10 and 7.

"Hello, I'm Grace," said the 10 year old girl.
"I'm Agnes," said the 7 year old girl.
"I'm Mary and this is Oliver," replied Mary.
"Have you come a long way?" asked Grace.
"About 100 miles," said Mary.
"That's a long way!" said Agnes.
"Come inside now," said their mother.
"We've got scones with jam," said Agnes.
"Is it strawberry jam?" asked Oliver.
"Yes," replied Grace.
"Brilliant!" shouted Oliver, beginning to smile.

Level 3 – Punctuation: Lesson 2 - Worksheet 1

Name: _____ Date: _____

Conversations

Correct the first conversation and then write one of your own.

A Country Walk

The next morning the children walked to the village.

Oliver was excited because he had never been to the countryside before.

What are those animals in the fields asked Oliver.

They are cows said Grace.

What's that yellow stuff in the fields asked Oliver.

It's wheat. It's made into flour and then into bread   replied Grace.

Then Oliver saw some trees. There were some red things hanging from the branches.

What are those things on the trees   asked Oliver.

Apples   answered Grace.

Wow! I didn't know they grew on trees shouted Oliver.

?

"

"

!

New Child in the Class:

_____

_____

_____

_____

_____

_____

Level 3 - Punctuation (Apostrophes - Belonging): Lesson 3

Writing Focus: Sentence Structure & Punctuation   **Theme:** Report

Target	To use apostrophes for belonging.
Resources	Worksheets, scissors, felt tip pens, 'Helping Hand' card (see page 64).
Warm Up	**Word Game** In twos, one person writes a word e.g. dog. Whatever the last letter is, the other person begins a word with it e.g. dog - gate - egg. Keep on going. Never write the same word twice.
Introduction	**Objective:** • Today we are going to look at how to use apostrophes. **By the end of the lesson:** • You will be able to use apostrophes for belonging correctly in you writing.
Remember	Reminder and reinforcement of key learning from previous lesson (if appropriate).
Model/Try	1. **What are Apostrophes?** Draw an apostrophe. Explain that we can use apostrophes to show when something belongs to one person even though the word used to describe that person ends in 's' e.g. 'the headteacher's room' tells us that room belongs to one headteacher. The apostrophe is used to show the room belongs to the headteacher. 2. **Worksheet 1: Text 1** Read the information. Highlight the apostrophes. Explain that if we didn't use apostrophes here, then the reader would think that there was more than one Jade, Mrs Mason, Iqbal, Lisa and Kelsey. N.B. Rather than explain all instances when apostrophes are used (which can result in a child putting apostrophes at the end of every plural), focus on apostrophes used to denote one person. This way the child will only use apostrophes for people's names. They can be taught at a later date other instances when apostrophes are used. 3. **Worksheet 1: Text 2** Read the information. There are lots of words ending in 's', but none of them need apostrophes. Remind them again that we use apostrophes when we write a plural of a person's name but want the reader to know that we are talking about only one person e.g. Adam's football boots. 4. **Worksheet 1: Text 3** Read the sentences. Highlight any words ending in 's.' Put in apostrophes only where they are needed i.e. Harry's, Farmer Brown's, Kelsey's, Dylan's and Mr Parker's
Apply	5. **Worksheet 2: Class Observations** Write some facts about children in your class using the table on the worksheet. Next write sentences where you compare two children and use two names, which will in turn need apostrophes. *e.g. Alice's hair is blonde but Ruby's hair is brown. Sam's favourite lesson is PE but Kara's favourite lesson is Music.*
Secure	6. Read your work out loud. Check that you have used apostrophes where they are needed.
Review & Reflect	7. On the 'Helping Hand' write several examples of when we use apostrophes for belonging.

Name: _____   Date: _____

Level 3 – Punctuation: Lesson 3 - Worksheet 1

Apostrophes for Belonging

Read the texts and discuss when to use an apostrophe to show belonging.

Discuss when to use apostrophes — Text 1

Jade's favourite game is hide and seek.

Mrs Mason's dog is a poodle.

Iqbal's football boots are very expensive.

Lisa's hair is black but Kelsey's hair is brown.

Discuss when not to use apostrophes — Text 2

Julia has a packet of crayons and two pens.

All the boys and girls are wearing hats and coats.

At lunch time Vasha ate six sandwiches and three cakes!

Where are my socks and shoes?

Put in the apostrophes — Text 3

Omar has one hundred marbles.

Harrys sister is an excellent artist.

My favourite pets are cats, dogs and rabbits.

In my pencil case I have two rubbers and three pencils.

Farmer Browns horses are black and grey.

Abdul stole the sweets out of my pocket.

Kelseys hair is neat but Dylans hair is messy.

I like Mr Parkers jokes.

© Topical Resources. May be photocopied for classroom use only.

Name: _____ Date: _____

Class Observations

Fill in the table and then write some facts about children in your class.

Name	Hair Colour	Eye Colour	Favourite Lesson	Favourite Food

Now write sentences comparing the children and using apostrophes.

Level 3 - Punctuation (Apostrophes - Contractions): Lesson 4

Writing Focus: Sentence Structure & Punctuation   **Theme:** Speech

Target	To use apostrophes for contractions
Resources	Worksheets, highlighter pens, 'Helping Hand' cards (see page 64).
Warm Up	**How Many?** How many reasons can you think of that your school is the best in town?
Introduction	**Objective:** • Today we are going to look at how to use apostrophes. **By the end of the lesson:** • You will be able to use apostrophes for contraction in your writing correctly.
Remember	Reminder and reinforcement of key learning from previous lesson (if appropriate).
Model/Try	1. **What are apostrophes?** Draw an apostrophe. Explain that we can use apostrophes to tell the reader where there are letters missing in a word. We use them because when we speak, we usually pronounce the words this way. Write some examples e.g. Don't = Do not. It's = It is. Ask the child to write the words and put in the apostrophe in the correct place. 2. **Worksheet 1: Speech** This is a speech written by a child. What is the speech about? – Answer: Sport in school. Read the speech out loud. Highlight the words with the contractions. Explain that each apostrophe takes the place of a letter e.g. don't = do not. Look at each word, which has an apostrophe. Highlight them. What letter does the apostrophe take the place of e.g. don't – letter 'o' is missing, there's – letter 'i' is missing. 3. **Worksheet 2: Prime Minister's Speech** Look at the list of words. Write the words as contractions e.g. It is – it's, He is – he's. Next, read the Prime Minister's speech out loud. Now read it replacing the words highlighted with contractions i.e. It's up to them how they spend their money.
Apply	4. **Worksheet 3: Write a Speech** Write a short speech about why children should have regular swimming lessons in school. Think of three reasons e.g. keeps them safe, keeps them fit, good fun. Write your speech including at least three contractions e.g. **It's** a great way of keeping fit.
Secure	5. Read your work out loud. Check that you have used at least three contractions.
Review & Reflect	6. On the 'Helping Hand' write several contractions which you would like to use in class.

Apostrophes for Contraction

Read the speech and highlight the contractions.

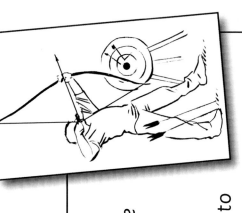

Abbey's Speech - Sport in Schools

I **don't** think that schools are given enough money to spend on sport. **That's** why we **didn't** do well in the last Olympics.

Firstly, **there's** not enough money for extra teachers. **It's** impossible for one teacher to teach individual sports like archery or judo to a class of children. **That's** why children have to play team games such as football or netball where they can all be involved at one time. **It's** no wonder we **don't** do well in individual sports!

Secondly, there **isn't** enough money for special equipment. Not only does it mean that schools **can't** play certain sports but the ones they do play, the pupils have to use old equipment such as damaged rounders bats or tennis racquets.

Finally, why should children with sporting talents have to join clubs outside school to improve their skills? Some of them **can't** afford it, which is unfair. This **shouldn't** be happening in a country like ours. If we want to do well in the next Olympics **we're** going to need more money!

Name: _____ Date: _____

Level 3 – Punctuation: Lesson 4 - Worksheet 2

Contractions

Write the contractions and then read the Prime Minister's speech.

Words	Contraction	Words	Contraction
it is	it's	should not	
he is		would not	
she is		was not	
is not		were not	
do not		are not	
has not		can not	
had not		we are	
have not		they are	
did not		that is	
could not		there is	

The Prime Minister's Speech

Sport in Schools

I believe that schools get enough money. **It is** up to them how they spend their money. So long as pupils play sport and are taught a variety of sports then **that is** up to the school. Head teachers should employ teachers with greater sporting skills or should employ coaches to do it. Therefore, **we are** not to blame for the fact that we **do not** do well at the Olympics. The schools **should not** waste their money on things they **do not** really need.

It's up to them how they spend their money!

We're not to blame!

© Topical Resources. May be photocopied for classroom use only.

Name: _____ Date: _____

Contractions

Write why children should have regular swimming lessons using at least three contractions.

School Swimming Lessons

Level 3 - Connectives (Time / Sequence): Lesson 1

Writing Focus: Sentence Structure & Punctuation   **Theme:** Story - Familiar Settings

Target	To use a range of connectives to signal time
Resources	Worksheets, scissors, 'Helping Hand' cards (see page 64).
Warm Up	**How Many?** How many words can you think of which rhyme with the word 'date' e.g. bait, crate, eight, fate, gate, great, hate, late, mate, plate, rate, skate, straight, state, wait, weight.
Introduction	**Objective:** • Today we are looking at connectives, which relate to time or a sequence. **By the end of the lesson:** • You will be able to write sentences using time/sequence connectives to link a story.
Remember	Reminder and reinforcement of key learning from previous lesson (if appropriate).
Model/Try	1. **Worksheet 1: Time Connectives** Cut out the connectives on Worksheet 1. Read the sequence connectives. Explain that sequence means an order. Explain that sequence connectives link one sentence to another. They help the reader understand how things happened and the order in which they happened. Without them a story can be difficult to understand. Write down the sequence connectives. 2. **Worksheet 2: Story 'The Broken Skateboard'** Read Text 1. Why is this a poor story? Answer: No time connectives linking the story together. Most sentences start with 'he' or 'then' which is not very interesting. Read Text 2. Why is this a good story? Time connectives link the story together, which make it more interesting. 3. **Worksheet 3:** Fill in the spaces in the sentences using time connectives.
Apply	4. **Worksheet 4: Story 'The Broken Bicycle'** Write your own story about a broken bicycle using Worksheet 4. Remember to use time connectives.
Secure	5. Underline the time connectives.
Review & Reflect	6. **Helping Hand Card** Write four time connectives onto the 'Helping Hand' card. Spell these connectives without looking.

25

Level 3 – Connectives: Lesson 1 - Worksheet 1

Cut out the time/sequence connectives.

The Broken Skateboard

Read and compare the two texts.

Text 1

Jack went fishing. He found a skate board. He took it home. He washed it. He dried it. He scraped off the old paint. He painted it. Then it rained so he went inside. He did not know that a wheel was loose. The next day Jack got up early. He set off for the skate park. Then he saw a bus at the bottom of the hill. He couldn't stop!

Text 2

One sunny afternoon Jack went fishing. While he was sitting on the river bank he saw a broken skate board in the reeds so he picked it up and took it home. **First** he washed off all the dirt. **Next** he scraped off the old paint with a wire brush. **Afterwards** he drew a fancy pattern on it. **Later** he painted the skate board in bright colours. **Not long after** it began to rain so he ran inside, not realising that one of the wheels was loose!

The next morning Jack woke up early. **First** he had breakfast. **Afterwards** he put on his helmet. **Finally**, he jumped on his skate board and set off down the road to the skate park. **Suddenly** Jack saw a double decker bus at the bottom of the hill but he couldn't stop!

Name: _____ Date: _____

Time Connectives

Fill in the spaces using appropriate time connectives.

Last week it was Mike's birthday so his parents took him out for a treat. _____ they went ten pin bowling. _____ they had tea in a restaurant. _____ they went to the cinema.

At the weekend the Robinson family went to the sea side. _____ they had a picnic on the beach. _____ they paddled in the sea. _____ they played cricket on the beach. _____ they went to the fun fair.

Name: _____ Date: _____

Level 3 – Connectives: Lesson 1 - Worksheet 4

The Broken Bicycle

Write your own story about a broken bicycle.

First · Next · Afterwards · In a while · Later · Not long after · Suddenly · Finally

One day	First	Next	Finally

© Topical Resources. May be photocopied for classroom use only.

Level 3 - Connectives (Subordinate Conjunctions): Lesson 2

Writing Focus: Sentence Structure & Punctuation   **Theme:** Non - Fiction Report

Target	To compose a complex sentence using a subordinate conjunction
Resources	Worksheets, highlighter pen, cube & 'Helping Hand' card (page 64).
Warm Up	**Word Game** How many words can you think of beginning with the letters 'sh' which have four letters or more? e.g. shop, ship, shed, shape, shall, shell, show, sheep, shine, share, should, shark.
Introduction	**Objective:** • Today we are looking at subordinate conjunctions. **By the end of the lesson:** • You will be able to write sentences using a variety of conjunctions in a report.
Remember	Reminder and reinforcement of key learning from previous lesson (if appropriate).
Model/Try	1. **Subordinate Conjunctions** Write down the subordinate conjunctions (listed below) onto a piece of paper - **before, if, when, although, instead of, unless**. Copy the words and say out loud. Explain that these words are subordinate conjunctions. We can use them at the beginning of sentences to make sentences more interesting. (We can also use them in the middle of sentences, but this can be taught in another lesson). 2. **Worksheet 1: Sentences or Not?** Look at the sentences on Worksheet 1. These sentences begin with subordinate conjunctions. Some of them are sentences but some of them are not. Read the examples. The first one is a sentence but the second one isn't because it is unfinished. Read the rest of the sentences and underline the subordinate conjunctions. Discuss which ones are sentences and which ones are not? Write yes or no then put a full stop if you think it is a sentence. Every sentence, which begins with a subordinate conjunction, has a comma after the first part of the sentence before it goes on to the main part of the sentence. The first part of the sentence will make the reader want to know what is going to happen next e.g. Although I like swimming ... We should use subordinate conjunctions in our writing because they make the reader want to carry on reading. 3. **Cube Game: Sentences** Write the six conjunctions onto a cube. Take it in turns to roll the cube and think of a sentence beginning with the conjunction the cube shows. 4. **Cube Game: What's Missing?** Now take it in turns to roll the cube to help you begin a sentence e.g. Although it was pouring with rain... Your partner must finish the sentence. Take it in turns to be the one who starts the sentence and the one who finishes it.
Apply	5. **Worksheet 2: All About Me** Write sentences about 'you' using subordinate conjunctions e.g. Although I like ice-lollies, I prefer ice cream. After I have done my homework I am allowed out to play. Rather than play football, I prefer to play cricket. Remember to use a comma at the end of the subordinate clause.
Secure	6. Colour the conjunctions using highlighter pen.
Review & Reflect	7. Write down five conjunctions on the 'Helping Hand' card which you would like to use in your writing.

Name: _____   Date: _____

Level 3 – Connectives: Lesson 2 - Worksheet 1

Sentences or Not?

Decide which of the following are sentences. Write YES or NO next to each one.

	Yes / No
Example: Although I like ice cream, I prefer ice lollies.	Yes
Example: Although I like swimming.	No
Before I go to bed, I clean my teeth.	
Before I get up.	
If I tidy my room, I get a treat.	
If I play with my baby sister.	
When I have had supper, I must go to bed.	
Although I like swimming.	
Instead of playing on the computer, I learn my spellings.	
Unless I take the dog for a walk, I can't play with my friends.	

© Topical Resources. May be photocopied for classroom use only.

Name: _____ Date: _____

All About Me

Write, in the boxes provided, sentences about 'you' using subordinate conjunctions.

| hobbies | family | favourite food | school |

Subordinate conjunction	Subordinate clause	Main clause
Example: Before	I go to school,	I have my breakfast.
Before	I	
After		
When		
Unless		
Although		
Instead of		

Level 3 - Connectives (Subordinate Conjunctions): Lesson 3

Writing Focus: Sentence Structure & Punctuation **Theme:** Narrative - Dilemma

Target	To compose a complex sentence using a subordinate clause
Resources	Worksheets, scissors, highlighter pens, Blu-Tac, 2 cubes and 'Helping Hand' card (page 64).
Warm Up	**Likes and Dislkes** Draw a line down a piece of paper. On the left hand side write a list of ten things you like and on the other, ten things you dislike e.g. Like – holidays, films, friends, chocolate etc. Dislike – spiders, snakes, getting up early, tidying my room etc.
Introduction	**Objective:** • Today we are looking at conjunctions & subordinate clauses. **By the end of the lesson:** • You will be able to write complex sentences using subordinate conjunctions to improve your writing.
Remember	Reminder and reinforcement of key learning from previous lesson (if appropriate).
Model/Try	1. **Subordinate Conjunctions** Write the list of conjunctions below onto a piece of paper or wipe board – **while, instead of, although, in case, if, rather than**. We can use these words to begin sentences and they are called subordinate conjunctions. The first part of the sentence makes the reader want to know what is going to happen next e.g. While he was walking home from school... We should therefore use them in our writing because they make the reader want to carry on. 2. **Worksheet 1: Choices** Read the sentences out loud on Worksheet 1 and highlight the conjunctions. Notice how the sentences are made of two parts (subordinate clause and main clause) Notice that every sentence, which begins with a subordinate conjunction, has a comma after the first part of the sentence before it goes on to the main part of the sentence. What happens if the second part of the sentence isn't there? Answer: It's no longer a sentence. 3. **Cube Games** On a cube write the six conjunctions you used in Worksheet 1. Take it in turns to roll the cube and think of a sentence beginning with that word. Next, take another cube. Cut up the dilemma pictures on Worksheet 2. Stick them on the cube. What dilemmas/choices are they? Take it in turns to roll the two cubes. Whatever they land on make a sentence e.g. Conjunction – Although, Picture – stealing. Although the child knew it was wrong, she stole some sweets from the shop.
Apply	4. **Worksheet 3: Dilemmas** Write your own dilemma sentences using different conjunctions.
Secure	5. Read through your sentences and underline the conjunctions. Highlight the commas.
Review & Reflect	6. Write down five subordinate conjunctions on the 'Helping Hand' card. 7. Spell the conjunctions without looking.

33

Name: _____ Date: _____

Choices

Read the sentences out loud and then highlight the conjunctions.

Good Choice | Bad Choice

Subordinate conjunction	Subordinate clause	Main clause
While	he was walking home from school,	Amrit saw some children playing knock and run.
Instead of	stealing sweets from the shop,	Hassan ran home.
Although	he knew it was wrong,	Danny swore at some boys from another school.
In case	he got in trouble from his mother,	Liam lied and said his sister had eaten all the cakes.
Rather than	learn her spellings for the test,	Anna copied Safi's spellings.
If	he bullies other children,	Mark will get into trouble.

Level 3 – Connectives: Lesson 3 - Worksheet 2

Dilemmas

Cut out the dilemmas and stick to the sides of a cube.

Name: _____ Date: _____

Choices

Write your own dilemma sentences using different conjunctions.

Good Choice | **Bad Choice**

Subordinate conjunction	Subordinate clause	Main clause

Level 3 - Connectives (Subordinate Conjunctions): Lesson 4

Writing Focus: Sentence Structure & Punctuation **Theme:** Report - Occupations

Target	To compose a complex sentence using subordinate conjunctions
Resources	Worksheets, scissors, 9 counters, 'Helping Hand' card (see page 64).
Warm Up	**Jobs** Write a list of occupations from A - Z e.g. A - artist, B - builder, C - chef, D - dentist or play a mime game where you act out an occupation and the other/s have to guess who it is.
Introduction	**Objective:** • Today we are looking at conjunctions & subordinate clauses. **By the end of the lesson:** • You will be able to write complex sentences using a variety of subordinate conjunctions to write a report.
Remember	Reminder and reinforcement of key learning from previous lesson (if appropriate).
Model/Try	1. **Worksheet 1: Three in a Row** Read all the subordinate conjunctions. Remind pupils that we can use these words to begin sentences to make them more interesting. Give example sentences using any conjunctions they are unsure of. Play three in a row in pairs. Don't write on the board game; use counters so that you can use the board repeatedly. Choose a subordinate conjunction. If you can think of a sentence e.g. 'When I am seventeen I will learn to drive', place a counter over the word. The next player then takes a turn to play. Get three counters in a row to win. 2. **Worksheet 2: When I Grow Up** Cut up the sentences on Worksheet 2. Arrange the sentences in their original order for the child/children to look at. Say aloud the conjunctions. Remind pupils that the main clause can stand alone as a sentence, but the part with the conjunction in it, cannot. Every sentence which begins with a subordinate conjunction needs a comma after the first part of the sentence before it goes on to the main part of the sentence. Place a comma where there is a natural break. Question: Why should we use these kinds of sentences? Answer: The first part of the sentence makes the reader want to know what is going to happen next. They add interest.
Apply	3. **Worksheet 3: Write a Report** Write a report about what you want to be when you grow up. Use a variety of conjunctions to start your sentences. Remember to use commas.
Secure	4. Read through the report aloud. Check that you have used commas where they should be used.
Review & Reflect	5. Spell as many subordinate conjunctions as you can. 6. Write any new conjunctions on your 'Helping Hand' card.

Name: _____ Date: _____

Subordinate Conjunctions
Three in a Row

Level 3 – Connectives: Lesson 4 - Worksheet 1

although	while	when
in case	before	unless
rather than	if	instead of

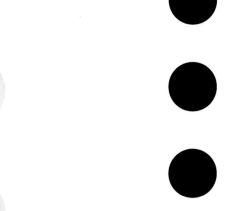

When I Grow Up

Cut up the sentences and arrange in the original order. Read each sentence and place a comma where there is a natural break. What do you notice?

Subordinate clause	Main clause
When I grow up	I would like to be an astronaut.
Before I become an astronaut	I will have to pass lots of exams
Instead of playing on my X Box every night	I am going to start reading books about space
Although it is an extremely dangerous job	I will be paid lots of money.
If I work really hard	I will be able to go to the moon in a space ship.

39

Name: _____ Date: _____

Level 3 – Connectives: Lesson 4 - Worksheet 3

When I Grow Up

Write a report about what you want do when you grow up. Use a variety of conjunctions to start your sentences.

When

Level 3 - Adjectives: Lesson 1

Writing Focus: Sentence Structure & Punctuation   **Theme:** Fiction – Imaginary Worlds

Target	To use adjectives to create detail, variety and add interest.
Resources	Worksheets, scissors, 'Helping Hand' card (page 64), four Adjective Cards (page 67).
Warm Up	How many words can you make out of the words 'space station' e.g. pat, pet, pit, pot, sat, sit
Introduction	**Objective:** • Today we are looking at adjectives and how we can use them in our writing. **By the end of the lesson:** • You will be able to recognise adjectives and know how to use them. You will be able to write a story set in an imaginary world using adjectives.
Remember	Reminder and reinforcement of key learning from previous lesson (if appropriate).
Model/Try	1. **What are Adjectives?** Cut up the adjective cards for settings and objects and put into two piles. Explain that these words are adjectives, which are describing words. We use them to describe nouns which are names of things e.g. snowy – snowy mountain. Look at the list of adjectives related to settings and then the list related to objects we would find in science fiction stories. Explain the meaning of any adjectives they do not know. 2. **Adjective Card Game** Turn the adjective cards face down. Take it in turns to turn one over and think of a sentence using the adjective. 3. **Worksheet 1: Story Board– Mission to Ice Planet** Read the storyboard 'Mission to Ice Planet' on Worksheet 1. Explain that this story is set in an imaginary world – another planet. Highlight the adjectives in heavy black text in the first part of the storyboard. Now find the rest. Extension: Act out the story while the teacher reads it. 4. **Worksheet 2: Story Map** Look at the story map related to the story 'Mission to Ice Planet'. Fill in the missing nouns and adjectives e.g. gigantic glacier, titanium skis. Then tell the story out loud using those words to help you.
Apply	5. **Worksheet 3/4: Story – Mission to Red Planet** Write your own story but this time set on a very hot planet. Use Worksheet 3 to help you plan the story. First explain what each landform is. Then child/children fill in the details on the story map writing exciting adjectives to describe each place e.g. red hot volcano and then think of what they could use to get past each place e.g. supersonic blaster (to flatten the sand). Now write your story on Worksheet 4.
Secure	6. Edit your story. 7. Underline the adjectives.
Review & Reflect	8. Write five new adjectives on the 'Helping Hand' card.

41

Name: _____ Date: _____

Mission to Ice Planet

Level 3 - Adjectives: Lesson 1- Worksheet 1

Highlight the adjectives used in this story.

The space ship landed. I put on my **special** helmet and picked up my **light** space pack. Then I pressed the exit button. The **heavy** door opened and I walked down the **narrow** steps. **Large** snowflakes fluttered down like feathers and a **strong** wind blew. This was Ice Planet and I had to explore it and report back to base.	First I came to a gigantic glacier, which stretched as far as the eye could see. The glacier was made of frozen ice, which was slippery so I put on my supersonic skis and quickly skied to the other side.	Next I came to a foggy plain. I looked through my powerful binoculars and ahead of me I could see jagged rocks of all shapes and sizes. It would take hours to walk around the rocks so I picked up my solar powered rock blaster and created a path, which I could follow.

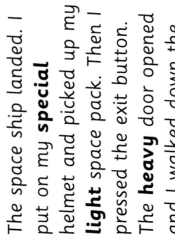

Soon I came to the snowy mountain. It was dangerous and steep so I used my pointed ice pick to help me climb to the top.

Finally I made my way back to the space ship. I turned on the engine. 3, 2, 1, Blast off! Another mission accomplished.

Name: _____ Date: _____

Mission to Ice Planet

Fill in the missing adjectives in the boxes.

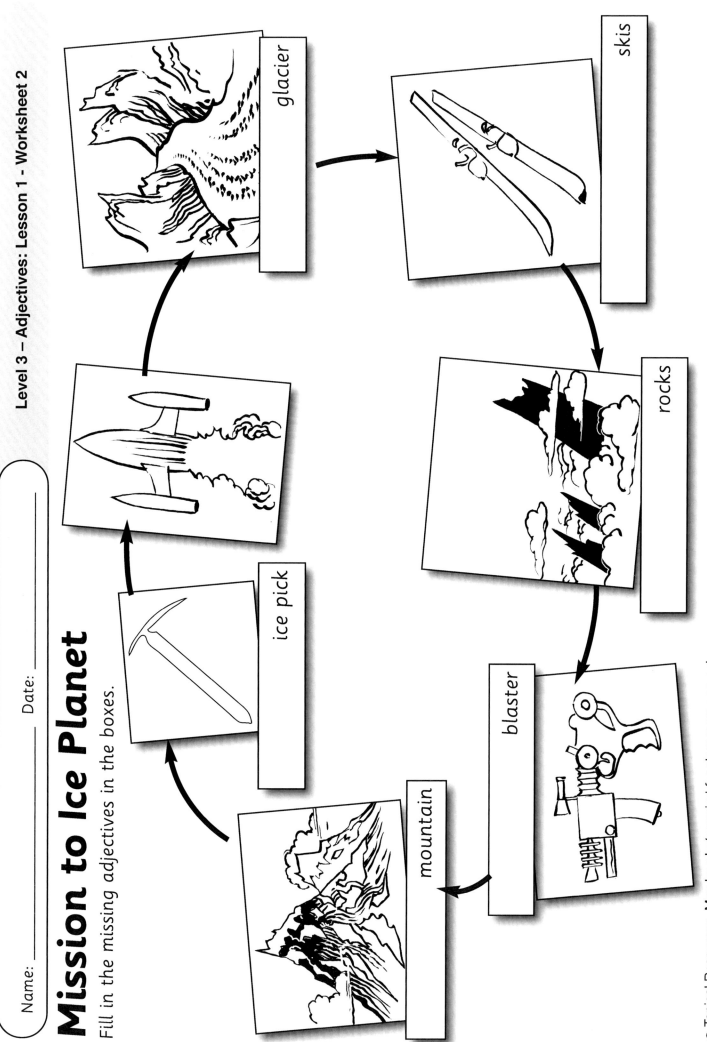

Level 3 – Adjectives: Lesson 1 - Worksheet 2

Name: _____ Date: _____

Mission to Red Planet

Fill in the missing tools to help you get past the different landscapes. Then use exciting adjectives to describe your nouns.

Name: _____   Date: _____

Mission to Red Planet

Level 3 – Adjectives: Lesson 1 - Worksheet 4

Write your own story about your mission to the Red Planet.

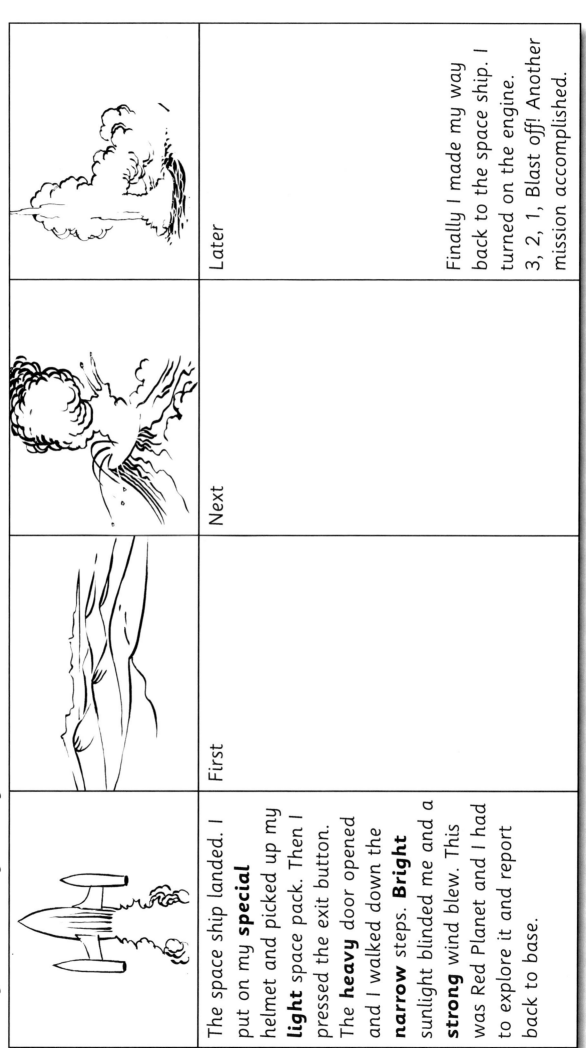

First

The space ship landed. I put on my **special** helmet and picked up my **light** space pack. Then I pressed the exit button. The **heavy** door opened and I walked down the **narrow** steps. **Bright** sunlight blinded me and a **strong** wind blew. This was Red Planet and I had to explore it and report back to base.

Next

Later

Finally I made my way back to the space ship. I turned on the engine. 3, 2, 1, Blast off! Another mission accomplished.

Level 3 - Adjectives: Lesson 2

Writing Focus: Sentence Structure & Punctuation   **Theme:** Non Fiction - Advertisement

Target	To use adjectives to create detail, variety and add interest
Resources	Worksheets, scissors, Adjective Cards (page 67) 'Helping Hand' card (page 64).
Warm Up	**Hangman** Play hangman using pets e.g. rabbit, horse. If the child cannot guess which pet it is, give them clues.
Introduction	**Objective:** • Today we are looking at adjectives and how we can use them in our writing. **By the end of the lesson:** • You will be able to recognise adjectives. • You will be able to use them in an advert to add detail, variety and interest.
Remember	Reminder and reinforcement of key learning from previous lesson (if appropriate).
Model/Try	1. **What are Adjectives** Cut up the adjective cards to describe people and pets. Use the ones, which are appropriate to the reading level and understanding of the child/children. Read the adjectives out loud. Explain that adjectives are describing words. We use them to describe nouns which are names of things e.g. dog, mountain etc. 2. **Worksheet 1: Pets for Sale** Read the two texts about pets for sale. You may see adverts like these in your local newspaper or on the internet. Which words are used to describe Jazz and Honey's personality? i.e. handsome, friendly etc. These words are called adjectives. Highlight them. When we use adjectives, the reader gets a clearer picture of what we are describing. All the adjectives in the texts are positive adjectives e.g. gentle, well behaved. There are no negative adjectives e.g. unfriendly, vicious. Question: Why are they positive and not negative? *Answer: Because no one would buy the pet if you said negative things about him or her.* 3. **Adjective Game** Using a cube, write on the faces six adjectives that the child/children are unfamiliar with e.g. curious, obedient etc. Explain the meanings of those adjectives. Take it in turns to roll the cube and whatever adjective the cube lands on, make up a sentence. 4. **A - Z of Adjectives** Write an A - Z of adjectives without looking at the adjective cards. How many can you think of? How many can you spell? Cross out any adjectives, which are negative e.g. vicious, naughty (as these words would not help you sell a pet).
Apply	5. **Worksheet 2: For Sale** Write your own 'For Sale' advert. Before you begin, choose some adjectives to describe your pet and write them on Worksheet 2 'Positive Adjectives'
Secure	6. Underline the adjectives you have used in your writing.
Review & Reflect	7. Write five new adjectives on the 'Helping Hand' card.

Name: _____ Date: _____

Level 3 – Adjectives: Lesson 2 - Worksheet 1

Pets for Sale

Highlight the adjectives used in these advertisements.

For Sale: Two Year Old Collie

Jazz is a handsome border collie looking for a new home because his family is moving to Australia.

He would make an ideal family pet because he is a friendly, gentle dog who likes children and adults. Jazz is an intelligent, obedient dog and he has been trained to do lots of exciting tricks. He is energetic and loves going for long walks where he will quite happily play fetch with balls and sticks. He has a soft bark and so he will not disturb the neighbours. You do not need to worry about him eating your best shoes or sitting on your expensive furniture because he is well behaved.

In just eight words, Jazz can be described as handsome, friendly, gentle, intelligent, obedient, energetic and well-behaved. Buy him now and you will have a friend for life.

For Sale: Three Month Old Rabbit

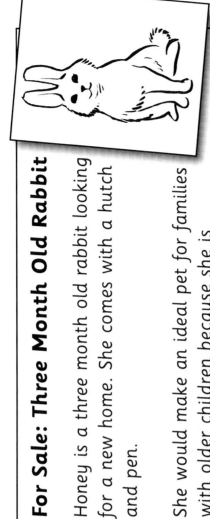

Honey is a three month old rabbit looking for a new home. She comes with a hutch and pen.

She would make an ideal pet for families with older children because she is affectionate and enjoys being picked up and stroked. She is good natured and never bites or scratches. Honey is lively and playful. She enjoys playing with balls and will even play fetch like a dog! Honey especially likes cardboard boxes which she can shred. She enjoys playing with paper which she can shred. She is energetic and likes running free around the garden. She is curious and loves exploring new places such as behind trees and bushes.

In just seven words, Honey can be described as affectionate, good-natured, lively, playful, energetic and curious. Buy her today and you will not be disappointed.

© Topical Resources. May be photocopied for classroom use only.

Level 3 – Adjectives: Lesson 2 - Worksheet 2

Name: _____ Date: _____

Pets for Sale

Write your own advertisement for a pet for sale.

My Positive Adjectives...

Level 3 - Adverbs: Lesson 1

Writing Focus: Sentence Structure & Punctuation **Theme:** Poetry – Familiar settings

Target	To use adverbs to add detail
Resources	Worksheets, scissors, 'Helping Hand' card (page 64), adverb cards (page 68).
Warm Up	**Alphabet animals** How many wild animals / zoo animals can you think of in five minutes?
Introduction	**Objective:** • Today we are looking at adverbs, how to recognise them and use them. **By the end of the lesson:** • You will be able to write sentences with adverbs to add detail to a poem.
Remember	Reminder and reinforcement of previous lesson (if appropriate).
Model/Try	1. **What are Adverbs?** Cut up the list of adverbs. Explain that an adverb is a word which describes a verb. Adverbs give the reader more information and make the picture clearer. They give us more detail. They tell us how something is done. How can we recognise them? They usually end in 'ly' e.g. swiftly, carefully. Read the adverbs. 2. **Game – Act it Out** Act out an adverb for another person to guess e.g. to act out the adverb 'slowly,' walk slowly across the room. Take it in turns to act out the adverb cards. 3. **Worksheet 1: Adverb Poem 'At the Zoo'** Read the poem on Worksheet 1. Highlight the adverbs. Pick up the adverb cards which have been used in the poem. Which adverbs are left? Can you think of sentences using the adverbs which are left? 4. **Worksheet 2: Circus** Look at the circus pictures on Worksheet 2. Have you ever been to a circus? What did you see? What acts can you see in the picture? Next read the adverbs. Draw a line matching an adverb to the circus act e.g. trapeze artist – bravely, clown – funnily. Find two adverbs for each circus act.
Apply	5. **Worksheet 3: Write your own poem** Write a poem about the circus using Worksheet 3. If the children have never been to a circus, watch a clip on' 'youtube', show them pictures in a book about the circus or download some pictures from the internet. On a piece of paper write a list of acts at the circus then match an act to an adverb e.g. happily – clowns, bravely – trapeze artist. Now write a poem beginning with an adverb about each act. You do not need to make the poem rhyme!
Secure	6. Read through the poem and edit. 7. Highlight the adverbs used.
Review & Reflect	7. Write five adverbs on the 'Helping Hand' card.

Adverbs

Read the poem and highlight the adverbs.

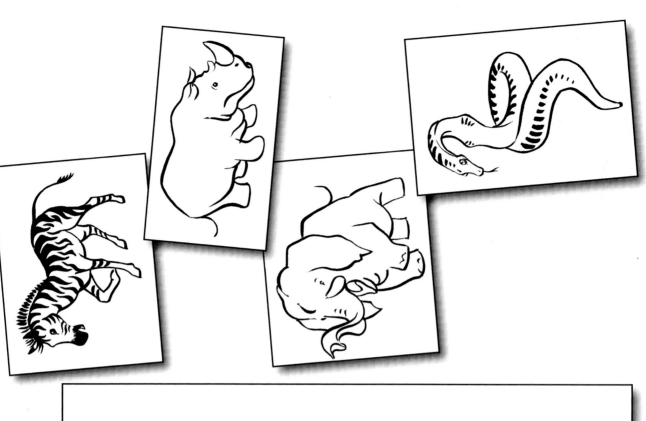

At the Zoo

Playfully the monkeys swing from branch to branch
Greedily the tiger tucks into his tea,
Obediently seals do their tricks with a ball
Shyly the panda peeps out from a tree.

Angrily the ape shows us all who's the boss
Cheerfully the elephant gives us a spray,
Quietly the meerkats run through the grass
Lazily the lion is sleeping all day.

Calmly the rhino gets up from his nap
Happily the zebras run to and fro,
Quickly the kangaroos leap far and wide
Slowly walks the camel with nowhere to go.

Beautifully the peacocks parade their feathers
Excitedly the penguins dive,
Silently the snakes slither and hiss
Cheekily the giraffes reach the leaves way up high.

Name: _____ Date: _____

Adverbs

Match the adverb to the circus act.

bravely

playfully

carefully

happily

nervously

calmly

obediently

funnily

Level 3 – Adverbs: Lesson 1 - Worksheet 2

Name: _____ Date: _____

Adverbs

Write a poem about the circus using adverbs to describe each act.

Level 3 - Adverbs: Lesson 2

Writing Focus: Sentence Structure & Punctuation **Theme:** Myths

Target	To use adverbs to add detail.
Resources	Worksheets, 'Helping Hand' card (page 64), adverb cards & verb cards (page 68)
Warm Up	**Bean Bag Game** In pairs throw a bean bag to each other and say a verb out loud. In two minutes how many verbs can you think of before you run out of ideas or say a word twice.
Introduction	**Objective:** • Today we are looking at adverbs. **By the end of the lesson:** • You will be able to write sentences with adverbs to add detail to our writing
Remember	Reminder and reinforcement of previous lesson if appropriate (Lesson 1 Adverbs)
Model/Try	1. **Reminder: What are Adverbs?** Reminder that an adverb is a word which describes a verb. It tells us how something is done. Adverbs usually end in 'ly' e.g. swiftly, carefully. Adverbs can improve our writing because they give the reader more information and make the picture clearer. 2. **Game: Matching Verbs to Adverbs** Cut up the adverb cards and powerful verb cards (pages 68). Turn the verb cards face down. Lay out the adverb cards so that you can see them all. Pick up a powerful verb e.g. tiptoed. Match the verb to an adverb e.g. tiptoed – quietly. Then think of sentence using those words with the adverb coming first e.g. Quietly, Tom tiptoed across the room. Next explain (using an adverb card and a verb card), that you do not need to place the adverb at the beginning of the sentence before the verb. You can place the adverb after the verb e.g. Tom tiptoed quietly across the room OR Tom tiptoed across the room quietly. Take it in turns to pick up a verb, match it to an adverb, then make up a sentence using those words so that the adverb comes after the verb. 3. **Worksheet 1: Matching Adverbs** Highlight the verbs. We can make the sentences more interesting by adding adverbs to describe the verbs. Using the adverb cards, choose an adverb to match each picture. Notice how the adverb comes after the verb. 4. **Worksheet 2: Greek Gods** Tell the child/children that you are going to read some information about Greek gods. In ancient Greece, the people believed in gods. The gods were very powerful and could do magical things. Read the information. Note that there aren't any adverbs. Explain that if we were going to write about the gods in a story, we could use adverbs to emphasise their powers and give the reader a clearer picture. Choose an adverb to go with each underlined verb.
Apply	5. **Worksheet 3: Greek Gods** Using the adverbs you have created on Worksheet 2, write a sentence about each of the Greek Gods. e.g. **Angrily**, Poseidon made storms which drowned fishermen. Pan danced **merrily** and **playfully** to the tune of the pipes.
Secure	6. Read through your writing and edit. Highlight the adverbs used.
Review & Reflect	8. Write five adverbs on the 'Helping Hand' card.

Adverbs Describe Verbs

Choose an adverb to describe each action.

The girl smiled _____

The dog sat _____

The boy fought _____

The girl swam _____

The baby slept _____

The mother brushed the child's hair _____

Name: _____ Date: _____

Greek Gods

Level 3 - Adverbs: Lesson 2 - Worksheet 2

Read the information about the Greek gods and write your own sentences using adverbs to describe the underlined verbs.

Poseidon was god of the sea. He was very bad tempered. Once when some sailors upset him, he _made_ a storm and they all drowned.

Pan was god of the shepherds. He had goat horns and feet. He _played_ the pipes. He _danced_ to the tunes.

Hercules was a warrior. He _killed_ scary monsters like Cerberus the three-headed dog.

Icarus wanted to fly so his father made him wings of feathers and wax. Icarus _flew_ too near the sun, his wings melted and he fell to his death!

Cyclops was a giant. He had one eye. He _ate_ human beings.

Minotaur had the body of a man and the head of a bull. He was imprisoned in a maze. He captured humans, _killed_ them and ate them.

© Topical Resources. May be photocopied for classroom use only.

Name: _____ Date: _____

Adverbs

Write a sentence about each Greek God beginning with an adverb.

Icarus

Poseidon

Cyclops

Hercules

Pan

Minotaur

Level 3 – Prepositions: Lesson 1

Writing Focus: Sentence Structure & Punctuation   **Theme:** Non Fiction - Description

Target	To use prepositions to add detail
Resources	Worksheets. 'Helping Hand' card (see page 64).
Warm Up	**Build a Story** Build a story word by word, in pairs, taking it in turn to add a word e.g. Once – upon – a – time – there – lived (orally or on paper).
Introduction	**Objective:** • Today we are looking at prepositions and how we can use them to add detail to our writing. **By the end of the lesson:** • You will be able to recognise prepositions and use them to write a description.
Remember	Reminder and reinforcement of key learning from previous lesson (if appropriate).
Model/Try	1. **Worksheet 1: Word Game** Cut up the prepositions on Worksheet 1. Read them out loud. Explain prepositions are the words that indicate location i.e. where something is. 2. **Worksheet 1: Picture Game - In the Attic.** Put the preposition cards in front of you. Look at the picture of the attic. In twos take it in turns to ask questions about the picture e.g. Where are the books? Answer the question using a preposition i.e. The books are **by** the television. 3. **Worksheet 2: Read the Texts - In the Bedroom.** These descriptions are written in the present tense i.e. now, as though they are actually happening. Which text do you prefer? Text 1. Why? It's more interesting. How does the writer make it more interesting? The writer uses prepositions to tell us where things are and nouns & adjectives to describe things. The writer also uses the five senses i.e. see, hear, touch, smell and taste. In text two the writer only writes about what he can see and he doesn't use any prepositions.
Apply	4. **Worksheet 3: Write a Description** Now write your own description of a room e.g. your classroom (Worksheet 3). First of all draw the objects and furniture on the side of the room you are going to concentrate on (choose just one wall). After that, write your description. Remember to: • Write it in the present tense • Use the five senses (what you can see, hear, touch, smell, taste). • Use different prepositions to describe where everything is located. e.g. There are some exercise books on the teacher's desk.
Secure	5. Read through your writing and highlight the prepositions.
Review & Reflect	6. Write five prepositions on the 'Helping Hand' card.

Name: _____   Date: _____

In the Attic

in	on
above	below
under	behind
by	along
between	next to
beside	opposite

Name: _____ Date: _____

Level 3 Prepositions: Lesson 1 Worksheet 2

In the Bedroom

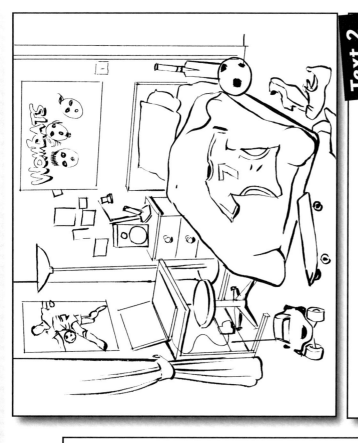

Text 1

I creep quietly into the room and feel the soft woollen carpet under my feet. This is my brother's bedroom and he doesn't know I'm here!

On his bed there is a football shirt with the number 7 on it. Above the bed there is a poster of a pop group and next to the bed there is a set of drawers. It has a shiny lamp on it and by the side of it is a small speaker for his stereo. Beside the bed there is a cricket bat, a football (which I bought him for his birthday) and a pair of new football boots. At the bottom of the bed there is a skateboard and next to it there is a remote controlled car.

Opposite the bed there is a computer table. On the table there is a new lap top. The lid is open and I can hear music playing. Under the table there is a round chair with a plastic seat. I sit on it and swivel all the way around. On the wall there is a large poster of a famous footballer.

Next to the table there is a tall window. The window is open and the blue curtains are billowing in the wind. The smell of freshly cut grass from outside tickles my nose. Behind the curtain is a glass jar. Inside the jar are some boiled sweets. I unscrew the lid and take one. It is very sticky but it tastes delicious. I wish this bedroom was mine!

Text 2

I walk into my brother's bedroom. I can see his bed and football shirt. There is a set of drawers with a lamp and speaker. I can see a cricket bat, football, football boots, skateboard and a remote controlled car. There is a computer table. I can see his lap top. The lid is open and music is playing. There is a round chair too. I can see a football poster. There are blue curtains in the window. The window is open. I can see a jar of sweets. I unscrew the lid and take a sweet.

© Topical Resources. May be photocopied for classroom use only.

Prepositions

Picture

in

by

on

above

below

between

opposite

behind

next to

beside

under

Level 3 - Noun Phrases: Lesson 1

Writing Focus: Sentence Structure & Punctuation   **Theme:** Narrative Openings

Target	To use adventurous word choices to engage the reader
Resources	Worksheets, scissors, 'Helping Hand' card (see page 64). Adjectives (page 67), Nouns (page 69)
Warm Up	**How Many?** How many words can you think of to put in front of the word cat e.g. hungry cat, tabby cat etc.
Introduction	**Objective:** • Today we are looking at using noun phrases. **By the end of the lesson:** • You will be able to use noun phrases in your sentences to make your writing more interesting.
Remember	Reminder and reinforcement of key learning from previous lesson. N.B. In order to complete this work effectively, you will need to have covered adjectives.
Model/Try	1. **Nouns** Cut up the noun cards. Explain that a noun is a name of something e.g. dog, man, car, book etc. A noun phrase can be a group of words around a noun, which give the noun more detail and make it more interesting for the reader. e.g. Instead of writing, 'The man,' which is not very interesting, we can add some words to it, to make it more interesting e.g. The old man with the wrinkly face.... A phrase is not a sentence. Today we are learning how to build up a phrase to make it more exciting. We are learning how to build a phrase before the noun and after the noun. 2. **Worksheet 1: Noun Phrases** Cut out the examples on Worksheet 1. Firstly, look at the phrases about kittens. Read the phrases one at a time, so that the child/children can see how the phrase is getting bigger and more interesting. Then the child/children can put the phrases about ice cream in order. Underline the noun i.e. ice cream. Look at how the phrases become more interesting as more words are added. 3. **Card Game (play in twos)** Cut up the adjective cards and lay them out so that you can see them all. Turn the noun cards face down. Turn one of the noun cards over e.g. beach. Add adjectives before and after the noun to make it more interesting e.g. beach - the sandy beach with the jagged rocks. Now extend the phrases and finish off to make a sentence e.g. The sandy beach with the jagged rocks was only a mile from my house.
Apply	4. **Worksheet 2: Write your own noun phrases** Choose two of the noun cards. Write your own noun phrases using your chosen words. Next, make them in to real sentences that could be the opening to a story.
Secure	5. Read your ideas out loud.
Review &	6. Write the types of words that can be added to a noun phrase to make it more interesting on the 'Helping Hand' card.

61

Name: _____ Date: _____

Adding Words to Improve Phrases

Level 3 - Noun Phrases: Lesson 1 - Worksheet 1

Read the phrases about kittens. Cut out the phrases about ice-cream and put in a similar order.

Kittens...

The cute **kittens**...

The cute, black **kittens**...

The cute, black **kittens** with pretty bows around their necks...

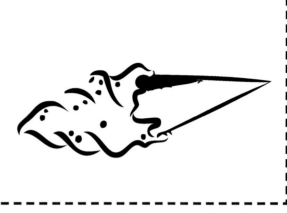

The tasty, vanilla ice cream...

Ice cream...

The tasty ice cream...

The tasty, vanilla ice cream with sprinkles on the top...

© Topical Resources. May be photocopied for classroom use only.

Name: _____ Date: _____

Adding Words to Improve Phrases

Choose nouns to write your own noun phrases. Turn them into the opening for a story by using a charact[...]

Character

1. _____

2. _____

3. _____

4. _____

Final sentence:

Setting

1. _____

2. _____

3. _____

4. _____

Final sentence:

Additional Resources *(enlarge if required)*

Helping Hands

Use the helping hand to help you remember what you have learned in the lesson. Write the heading in the middle of the hand and then the words associated with it on the fingers. Cut out the hand and attach each subsequent hand using a paper fastener. See the example above.

Cube Template

Additional Resources *(enlarge if required)*

Irregular Verbs - Present Tense

say	send	sell	spread	stick	throw	wake	
sing	see	sleep	speak	stand	think	take	
ride	sit	shake	spend	steal	swim	tell	write

Irregular Verbs - Present Tense

break	catch	eat	feel	forget	grow	know	lie	read
buy	come	drive	feed	fly	go	hear	lose	run
begin	bring	drink	fall	find	give	have	leave	make

Additional Resources *(enlarge if required)*

Irregular Verbs - Past Tense

said	sent	sold	spread	stuck	threw	woke	
sang	saw	slept	spoke	stood	thought	took	
rode	sat	shook	spent	stole	swam	told	wrote

- -

Irregular Verbs - Past Tense

broke	caught	ate	felt	forgot	grew	knew	lied	read
bought	came	drove	fed	flew	went	heard	lost	ran
began	brought	drank	fell	found	gave	had	left	made

Additional Resources *(enlarge if required)*

Adjectives

Adjectives to describe settings

sunny	rainy	windy
chilly	frozen	icy
snowy	steep	slippery
dangerous	hot	boiling
scorching	sandy	rocky
bright	jagged	foggy

Adjectives to describe objects

heavy	light	large
special	strong	sharp
powerful	pointed	supersonic
electronic	x ray	solar powered

Adjectives to describe people and pets

active	adorable	adventurous
affectionate	athletic	beautiful
clever	cuddly	curious
cute	energetic	friendly
funny	furry	gentle
good natured	handsome	happy
large	lively	loving
obedient	playful	quiet
shy	small	smart
soft	strong	well-behaved

Additional Resources *(enlarge if required)*

Verbs

Verbs (Powerful)

walked	crawled	slipped
jogged	crept	skidded
rushed	leapt	tripped
raced	escaped	hobbled
sprinted	climbed	limped
hurried	tiptoed	jumped
dashed	marched	travelled

- -

Adverbs

Adverbs tell us how we do something

angrily	beautifully	bravely
calmly	carefully	cheerfully
cheekily	excitedly	funnily
gently	greedily	happily
lazily	merrily	nervously
noisily	obediently	peacefully
playfully	politely	quickly
quietly	sadly	selfishly
shyly	silently	sleepily
slowly	stupidly	viciously